MW01029215

QUEEN

OF A

RAINY

COUNTRY

Also by Linda Pastan

QUEEN
OF A
RAINY
COUNTRY

LINDA PASTAN

W. W. NORTON & COMPANY

NEW YORK   LONDON

Copyright © 2006 by Linda Pastan

All rights reserved
Printed in the United States of America
First Edition

For information about permission to reproduce selections from this book, write to
Permissions, W. W. Norton & Company, Inc., 500 Fifth Avenue, New York, NY 10110

Manufacturing by The Courier Companies, Inc.
Book design by Georgia Liebman
Production manager: Andrew Marasia

Library of Congress Cataloging-in-Publication Data

Pastan, Linda, 1932–
Queen of a rainy country / Linda Pastan. — 1st ed.
p. cm.
ISBN-13: 978-0-393-06247-2
ISBN-10: 0-393-06247-3
I. Title.
PS3566.A775Q84 2006
811'.54—dc22

2006009081

W. W. Norton & Company, Inc., 500 Fifth Avenue, New York, N.Y. 10110
www.wwnorton.com

W. W. Norton & Company Ltd., Castle House, 75/76 Wells Street, London W1T 3QT

1 2 3 4 5 6 7 8 9 0

In Memory of My Father

Contents 🌱

ACKNOWLEDGMENTS

I would like to thank the following magazines in which many of these poems first appeared:

The Atlantic Monthly, Botteghe Oscure, The Georgia Review, The Gettysburg Review, The Hampton–Sydney Poetry Review, Inertia, The Kenyon Review, Margie, The Nation, Natural Bridge, New Letters, The Paris Review, Poet Lore, Poetry, Poetry International, Prairie Schooner, Shenendoah, The Southern Poetry Review, Sycamore, Washingtonian, Washington Square, The Western Humanities Review, Witness.

"Death Is Intended" appears in *Best American Poetry 2004.*

I

A Tourist at Ellis Island

I found him, Jankel Olenik,
age 3, on the manifest
of the ship Spaarndam
in 1902—my surgeon father
Jack, of the silk ties
and trimmed mustache,
who never mentioned
the life he once inhabited
not just in a different language

but in a different book,
its pages yellowed at the edges.
He thrust me into the new world
scrubbed clean of peasant dirt,
whole chapters of my history
torn out. Failed
archeologist of memory,
I never asked
a single question.

Maiden Name

My daughter's teacher is named
Olenik—my maiden name,
and Olenik was the name of a therapist
I talked to once about my dread of lightning—
I finally bought a lightning rod instead.
There's even a Russian poet who spells
his name with a *c* instead of a *k*
but may share my taste
for melancholy, my ice-blue Slavic eyes.
Are we defined by names, or
was Adam merely arbitrary, pointing
at some wooly creature and legislating: lamb?
I was never really a maiden anyway,
not the way I like to think of that word—
Rapunzel or the milkmaids in Elizabethan lyrics,
and I haven't used Olenik in fifty years.
But hearing that name spill out again so casually
from my daughter's shapely Olenik mouth
is like waking up after a too-long sleep
and having to rub the syllables from my eyes.

To My Imaginary Siblings

Dear brother and sister,
you who helped me survive
the bleakness of my only childhood,
who were as real to me then
as the characters in my thumbed-over books:
are you grown now? Did one of you become
a surgeon, like our father, and do you both
still mirror our mother's severe beauty
which I endowed you with,
even though it passed me by?
I had my children early, thinking
they would be like my own siblings,
and though they never were,
in the busy boredom of domesticity,
I somehow left the two of you behind.
If you were still around, would we chat
on the phone each morning in the warmth
of our separate cups of coffee?
Or would we have quarreled by now
over which of us was the more loved
or over what our parents left us?
Would I have had to give one of you our mother's
opal stickpin and the other the two lusterware jugs
that sit in my kitchen now, remnants
of our childhood home—that antique house
where in the secular heaven of the remembered
family, you are simply two more ghosts?

PARTING THE WATERS

Nothing is lost.
The past surfaces
from the salted tide pool
of oblivion over
and over again,
and here it is now—
complete
with ironed sheets, old sins,
and pewter candlesticks.
My mother and aunts approach,
shaking the water from
their freshly washed hair
like aging mermaids.
They have been here
all along, sewing
or reading a book, waiting
for the wand of memory
to touch them.

A Boy

A boy my husband hired
is cutting the grass,
his white T-shirt glowing
like a friendly ghost as evening

catches up with him.
If I half close my eyes
it could be one of my sons
grown back to boyhood,

pushing a mower
through the fading light,
the green blades falling
like years under his feet.

THE PHOTOGRAPHER
IN MEMORY OF TOM VICTOR

It wasn't my soul he captured
in his intricate box
but his idea of the poet
as beautiful woman. He ran ahead
kneeling in front of me,

a seductive supplicant murmuring:
"lovely, lovely . . . turn
your head a little . . . lick your lips,"
as if he were instructing me
in the myriad gestures of love.

And in those moments
I became beautiful for him,
you can see it in the finished photograph
which rose like Venus
from its bath of chemicals.

When I look at that picture now I see
a woman with widened eyes, a fan
of hair, iconic cheekbones,
a woman quite different
from the plain one I see

in the mirror every day.
I was transformed as language itself
is transformed and quivers in a poem, though
the words themselves, taken separately,
would seem quite ordinary.

Anomaly

No one has a heart like yours
the doctor tells me, studying
the CT angiogram with barely
concealed excitement—

an explorer in white
discovering a tropical island—
exotic foliage instead of
the body's usual geography.

And he shows me the picture
of my heart proudly, one artery
instead of two snaking from the aorta,
dividing only later

into tributaries that nourish
this aging body: white cells
and red cells paddling madly
towards the organs on shore.

Oh uncharted rivers of blood!
Why am I heartsick, heartsore,
heavy hearted? Haven't I always known
my heart was different?

Geography

I am haunted by the names
of foreign places: Lvov and its bells;
Galway with its shimmer of green;
Grudnow and Minsk
where my grandfather's famished face
belongs on the tarnished coins.

I am haunted by the weight of all those histories:
coronations and christenings; massacres,
famines—people shoveled
under the dark earth, just so much compost,
the lowly potato failing in Ireland,
like daylight itself failing at noon.

Oh, the vastness of maps,
the perfect roundness of globes—
those bellies pregnant with the names
of unimaginable townships and cities. Atlantis
and the Isles of the Blest are not as haunting to me
as Guangzhou or Xi'an or Santorini.

A for Ancona, an operator intones,
N for Napoli, T for Turino,
and at her voice longitudes and latitudes
become entangled like fishnets, waves
of people migrate across borders and oceans
and through the teeming streets of Buenos Aires.

While I remain quietly here in my anonymous woods
where the stream beyond the kitchen window
is so small it is only visible when it creams to ice,
where even in spring, resurgent with rain,
all it can do is empty itself into another stream,
also small, also nameless.

In Another Country

Cernobbio, Sunday Morning

The trick is to leave yourself behind,
to disguise yourself
in the unselfconscious body
of a woman you always meant to be,
to sip a glass
of prosecco in the sun
like sipping the sun itself.
I pluck the petals
of a dozen daisies and always get
the same answer; but here
where language consists
not of words but of syllables of music,
no answer matters.
There are only flowers.
There is only the lake, concealing
in its blueness the drowned
gates of that first vineyard.
And we are still locked safely in,
the wine somehow alive
in every glass, our tickets home,
like the angel's final summons,
no more for now
than the mother of beauty.

The Life I Didn't Lead

took place in Italy:
black figs and gilded apricots;
a clatter of bells;
the vivid repartee of birds
as migratory as I was.
Or in Paris with its classical maze
of buildings and bridges
where French perfected itself
in my mouth, already lush
with wine and bruised with kisses.
A flute of chilled champagne
each morning... that beautiful
Belgian boy each afternoon...
a single yellow rose became
my long-stemmed bookmark.
I learned the world the way
some women learn their kitchens—
all those unswept alleys, the scoured look
of deserts, the knife-edged borders
between men and countries.
And time went by so slowly,
and so fast, a river
whose source is hidden high
in the curve of a mountain:
freeze and frantic meltdown
and freeze again.
Like pebbles in that riverbed
there were perfect
children along the way
and poems from time to time.
But the art that mattered
was the life led fully,
stanza by swollen stanza.

IN THE WALLED GARDEN

In the walled garden
where my illusions grow,
the lilac, watered, blooms all winter,
and innocence grows like moss
on the north side of every tree.
No ax or mower resides here—
green multiplies unimpeded—
and every morning all the dogs
of my long life jump up
to lick my face.
My father rests behind a hedge,
bard of my storied childhood,
and in the fading half-life of ambition,
wanting and having merge.
Here flowers and flesh don't wither.
Here you will never leave me.
Here poetry will save the world.

THINGS I DIDN'T KNOW I LOVED:
AFTER NAZIM HIKMET

I always knew I loved the sky,
the way it seems solid and insubstantial at the same time;
the way it disappears above us
even as we pursue it in a climbing plane,
like wishes or answers to certain questions—always out of reach;
the way it embodies blue,
even when it is gray.

But I didn't know I loved the clouds,
those shaggy eyebrows glowering
over the face of the sun.
Perhaps I only love the strange shapes clouds can take,
as if they are sketches by an artist
who keeps changing her mind.
Perhaps I love their deceptive softness,
like a bosom I'd like to rest my head against
but never can.

And I know I love the grass, even as I am cutting it as short
as the hair on my grandson's newly barbered head.
I love the way the smell of grass can fill my nostrils
with intimations of youth and lust;
the way it stains my handkerchief with meanings
that never wash out.

Sometimes I love the rain, staccato on the roof,
and always the snow when I am inside looking out
at the blurring around the edges of parked cars
and trees. And I love trees,
in winter when their austere shapes
are like the cutout silhouettes artists sell at fairs
and in May when their branches

are fuzzy with growth, the leaves poking out
like new green horns on a young deer.

But how about the sound of trains,
those drawn-out whistles of longing in the night,
like coyotes made of steam and steel, no color at all,
reminding me of prisoners on chain gangs I've only seen
in movies, defeated men hammering spikes into rails,
the burly guards watching over them?

Those whistles give loneliness and departure a voice.
It is the kind of loneliness I can take in my arms, tasting
of tears that comfort even as they burn, dampening the pillows
and all the feathers of all the geese who were plucked to fill
them.

Perhaps I embrace the music of departure—song without lyrics,
so I can learn to love it, though I don't love it now.
For at the end of the story, when sky and clouds and grass,
and even you my love of so many years,
have almost disappeared,
it will be all there is left to love.

II

Don't Think of This

Don't think of this as a final meal.
Concentrate on the taste of the food,
the salad so crisp (young lettuces they say)
the wine so potent, so sure of itself in the glass,
it can make us young for this one night.
The air outside is no different
from the air the first night we met—
that stroll through autumn
when our life together was not even a wish,
much less a design, and we could still
walk away into separate lives,
like parallel universes in a science fiction story—
our children, now grown, no more than shadows
in some book, outlined but never written.
There isn't much time left;
the waiter is clearing the table
as if of the debris of years.
But there is still a bed waiting with pillows
as yielding as passing clouds,
and we can sink into their whiteness
as though an endless stream of mornings
still waited to dawn ahead of us.

Par Avion

Dear Friend. I have slept
for many years in the shadow
of your body, treading with you
the swirling waters of sleep.
Now in the shattered light
of a single morning you fly off,
leaving behind the skeletal rattle
of empty hangers, your orchids
blooming their hearts out at the window,
and me who must anchor this house
to the fragrant earth alone.
The world beckons
with its singular temptations,
but I will not accommodate
such absence. Come back soon.

4 A.M.

What blandishments the world offers:
the hook, the gun, the coated pill,
anything to crack the darkness,
to still the air so resonant
with unplayed music. Somewhere
down the hall a red exit light
blinks and beckons me.
I hold my breath.

Still, I am heavy in my bones,
weighted here, my blood
making its ordinary rounds
down narrowing pathways.
Now the moon comes out,
a rag of light at the window.
Now the rhythmic music starts again:
the breathing out, the breathing in.

A Perilous Safety:
Anniversary Letter

This 48th milestone feels
like a joke, a millstone maybe,
or just an excuse—
as if we needed one,
for another good meal,
for haven't we
been feasting for years
on each other's company
and soon to be
failing flesh?

Last week
when that interviewer
asked me to list all the good things
about being in my sixties
and I couldn't come up with
even one,
she thought I was joking,
but I was dead
serious.
She wanted to know
the secret of such
a long marriage,

and though I shrugged and
said to myself: "dumb luck,"
I also thought: I have dared to dare little;
simplicities of sun and shade
have claimed me.

But sometimes looking up
at a blind white sky I will think
I have done everything
wrong, have risked any hope
of a heavenly city on earth
for what is really a perilous safety.

And so, I must
learn continually,
or we both must learn, or
we both are learning still
that passion is more
than a conflagration.
It can be a rage
of coals, each burning
in the blackened grate
with no brief promises
of flame, just this slow
and steady heat.

MARRIAGE

He is always turning the radio on,
or the stereo, or the TV news,
and she is always shouting at him
through the noise to turn them off.

It's the kind of thing that should be settled
before a marriage, the way prospective
college roommates must say whether they smoke.
But they've been together for years,

and he still fills his head with facts
and music (arias, average rainfalls,
the temperament of the nation) as if
he's saving them up for something.

She says it's like living with a flock
of angry crows, squawking and rattling
their wings inside the house.
She wants her head to be filled

with silence, with empty space
for tranquility to enter. There are times
when their life is a dance they perform
around each other, trying not to collide.

"Move the way a violin would sound,"
a real dancer said. He puts on her favorite
CD, a Brahms intermezzo.
Sometimes even crows are happy.

BEETHOVEN'S QUARTET IN C MAJOR, OPUS 59

The violins
are passionately
occupied, but
it is the cellist

who seems to be
holding the music
in his arms,
moving his bow

as if it were
a dowsing rod
and the audience
dying of thirst.

In Our Sculpture Garden

My husband takes the wooden statue
of Eve in his arms and wrestles it
to the other side of the deck. Does he
take pleasure in her acquiescence,
appreciating a woman
whose only resistance
is her inflexible weight?

I like to watch his muscles move
like a hidden constrictor
under his shirt (how would it be
to be manhandled like that?)
While Adam, no more than
the carved trunk of a tree himself,
watches blindly and waits his turn.

All I Want to Say

"A painter can say all he wants to with fruit or
flowers or even clouds."—Edouard Manet

When I pass you this bowl
of Winesaps, do I want to say:
here are some rosy spheres
of love, or lust—emblems
of all the moments after Eden
when a pinch of the forbidden
was like spice on that first apple?
Or do I simply mean: I'm sorry,
I was busy today; fruit is all
there is for dessert.

And when you picked
a single bloom from the fading bush
outside our window,
were you saying that I am somehow
like a flower, or deserving of flowers?
Were you saying
anything flowery at all?
Or simply: here is the last rose
of November, please
put it in water.

As for clouds,
as for those white, voluptuous
abstractions floating overhead,
they are not camels or pillows
or even the snowy peaks
of half-imagined mountains.
They are the pure shapes
of silence, and they are
saying exactly
what I want to say.

I Married You

I married you
for all the wrong reasons,
charmed by your
dangerous family history,
by the innocent muscles, bulging
like hidden weapons
under your shirt,
by your naive ties, the colors
of painted scraps of sunset.

I was charmed too
by your assumptions
about me: my serenity—
that mirror waiting to be cracked,
my flashy acrobatics with knives
in the kitchen.
How wrong we both were
about each other,
and how happy we have been.

LATE AFTERNOON, ST. JOHN

A little blue heron has landed
on the roof.
It is as if a small angel had parked
in our lives, shielding us
briefly with its wings.
In the cove the old turtle
surfaces again; shadows
of reef fish shiver by.
On the stones chameleons
go through their wheel of colors.
Rustle of coconut fronds
combing the soft air . . . glitter
of passing raindrops.
Let go. Let go.
Soon the sun will plunge
into the sea dragging its plumage
of pinks and purples.
I can almost taste
the oleander, smell
the salt on your skin.
Soon we will drown
in our five exploding senses.

50 Years

Though we know
how it will end:
in grief and silence,
we go about our ordinary days
as if the acts of boiling an egg
or smoothing down a bed
were so small
they must be overlooked
by death. And perhaps

the few years left, sun drenched
but without grand purpose,
will somehow endure,
the way a portrait of lovers endures
radiant and true on the wall
of some obscure Dutch museum,
long after the names
of the artist and models
have disappeared.

III

To Speak in Tongues

To speak in tongues
is simply to follow desire
out of the door of the mouth
and into the open air—that place
where language is seldom
understood. They will bring
doctors and interpreters
who will shake their heads
before they move on.
Soon even words will fade,
as stars must do at noon.
There are no choices here.

Alphabet Song

Like a train made up of 26 boxcars,
the alphabet drags such a heavy cargo
down the tracks, such strange,
compelling combinations

that we are left breathless, admiring
a world constructed of words
and sentences as much
as the sunsets and snowfalls

which perform their mysteries
before our distracted eyes.
Now we learn how alphabets of genes
produce jellyfish and roses

and the intricate brain
that invented language—then wrote
a poem which like a brief breeze
wafts over us and is gone.

The Art of Pain

The pain we feel reading
mere words in a book
clings to us like static
on a cold day. The road
a woman walks in the last chapter
twists away from her happiness,
and the pain follows
wherever we go, haunting us
with its mute footsteps—the ghost
of pain we have known

and of pain to come.
Small explosions
of grief in a sonnet sequence;
another fracture of innocence:
these are templates into which our lives
must fit themselves, moving shadows
the sun makes, rising and going down
on every page, as evening settles
into all the unswept corners
of the world.

Poems for Sale

"poems for sale, all occasions . . ."
—AD ON THE INTERNET

There are poems for sale,
sonnets and villanelles,
poems for all occasions:
a wedding or funeral
or a school assignment.
There are rhymed poems
(a little more expensive)
or free verse rambling over the page.
There is even a genuine haiku
(see the dragonfly
alight on the bird feeder,
eyeing the squirrel).
There are rosy love poems to lull
your love into bed and intricate
narratives to keep him there;
lyrics with snow falling into the margins
and couplets embracing
like long lost friends.
How I would like to purchase
a brand-new poem,
crinkling in its pastel tissue,
instead of sitting here
with a leaking pen whose blots
are the only marks on the paper
so far. If only I could decide
which poem to buy.
If only I didn't think the elegy
was meant for me.

READING POETRY TO CHILDREN
AT CROWNPOINT

The mountains here have suffered
everything—winds of the centuries passing
with their weight of snow, of fleeting rain;
what the fist of the sun can do.

Rusted down to red hills,
they are as creased and angular
as the Navajo grandmother's face which stared
impassively back at me this morning

across all the old frontiers.
Perhaps like the lovesick coyote disguised
as a young brave, a poem of mine
can blunder through to you.

On Seeing My Poems Translated into Chinese

This is the geometry
of pure design—
the intricate patterns
gulls' feet leave
on the clean sand;
the flutter of inked eyelashes
on a white cheek;
the coded scrawl
of kindergarten children.

What do these poems mean?
somebody always asks,
and I can open
the book here and point,
thinking of how Li Po once fished
in the river of language,
whose poems still glisten
wetly, even in English,
all the way down the page.

For the Sake of the Poem

For the sake of the poem
the bed remains disheveled all day,

the dishes loll in the sink
like adolescents. For the sake

of the poem a forest is cut down
to appease my appetite for paper.

A lover is betrayed in print;
hot tea and desire must

cool their heels,
for the sake of the poem.

I am an addict who needs
her daily fix of language.

Children are left uncombed;
unwatered, plants languish.

For the sake of the poem
old age is put on hold.

What wouldn't I do
for the sake of the poem?

"What Does Poetry Save You From?"

From the pale silence
of morning and the din
of afternoon.

From the flight into darkness
of those I continue
to love.

From my inarticulate body
and the syllables
that clog my mouth.

From having to say
"nothing," when a stranger
asks me what I do.

From my worst sins.
From the failure
of any other absolution.

Firing the Muse

I am giving up the muse Calliope.
I have told her to pack up her pens and her inks
and to take her lyrical smile,
her coaxing ways, back to Mt. Helicon,
or at least to New York.
I will even write her a reference if she likes
to someone whose head is still fizzy
with iambs and trochees,
someone still hungry for the scent of laurel,
the taste of fame, for the pure astonishment of seeing
her own words blaze up on the page.
Let me lie in this hammock in the fading sun
without guilt or longing, just a glass
of cold white wine in one hand,
not even a book in the other. A dog
will lie at my feet who can't read anyway,
loving me just for myself, and for
the biscuit I keep concealed in my pocket.

Rereading Frost

Sometimes I think all the best poems
have been written already,
and no one has time to read them,
so why try to write more?

At other times though,
I remember how one flower
in a meadow already full of flowers
somehow adds to the general fireworks effect

as you get to the top of a hill
in Colorado, say, in high summer
and just look down at all that brimming color.
I also try to convince myself

that the smallest note of the smallest
instrument in the band,
the triangle for instance,
is important to the conductor

who stands there, pointing his finger
in the direction of the percussions,
demanding that one silvery ping.
And I decide not to stop trying,

at least not for a while, though in truth
I'd rather just sit here reading
how someone else has been acquainted
with the night already, and perfectly.

IV

Heaven

Are there seasons in heaven?
In God's anteroom are there windows
that look out on trees like these—

each leaf a note for the brass
ensemble of autumn—
the dry ones castanets

clicking: October, October.
Can heaven itself be golden
enough to rival all this?

OCTOBER

No more than a few
blue shadows
move over it—
the merest hint
that gold is about
to tarnish and
the whole leafy carapace
of summer vanish
in smoke. Without
the seasons, we could be
as oblivious
as animals, for whom
death comes
without prefiguring
and only once.

Stained Glass October

You edge the flower beds
with your spade until the line
between the black earth
and the grass, so brilliantly green,

is as strict and straight as the leading
between panes of stained glass windows.
Who would expect autumn
to seem so medieval—the sun

spilling through colored leaves
as through the cathedral window in France
where our artist friend once lectured us—
that panel there, she said

(the peacock blue of the sky
today) represents the cloak of The Virgin.
If there were music now,
I think it would be trumpets.

And if the air were really wine,
we would sip it slowly—
old port, perhaps, the very color
of these maples turning.

The Death of the Self

Like discarded pages
from the book
of autumn, the leaves
come trembling down

in red and umber,
each a poem
or story,
an unread letter.

Think of the fires
in ancient Alexandria,
the voluminous smoke
of parchment burning.

Open your arms
to the dying colors,
to the fragile
beauties

of November.
Deep in the heart
of buried acorns,
nothing is lost.

November Rain

How separate we are
under our black umbrellas—dark
planets in our own small orbits,

hiding from this wet assault
of weather as if water
would violate the skin,

as if these raised silk canopies
could protect us
from whatever is coming next—

December with its white
enamel surfaces; the numbing
silences of winter.

From above we must look
like a family of bats—
ribbed wings spread

against the rain,
swooping towards any
makeshift shelter.

INTERLUDE

We are waiting for snow
the way we might wait for a train
to arrive with its cold cargo—
it is late already, but surely
it will come.

We are waiting for snow
the way we might wait
for permission
to breathe again.

For only the snow
will release us, only the snow
will be a letting go, a blind falling
towards the body of earth
and towards each other.

And while we wait at this window
whose sheer transparency
is clouded already
with our mutual breath,

it is as if our whole lives depended
on the freezing color
of the sky, on the white
soon to be fractured
gaze of winter.

SNOWED IN

white migraine
soft white paws under
the door of winter

pale fur
bleached feathers
drifting in

the phone dead
the trees bent
to breaking

white
all the children
of white

the porcelain sky
is breaking
to bits

March Snow

There is something hopeful about March,
something benevolent about the light,

and yet wherever I look snow
has fallen or is about to fall, and the cold

is so unexpected, so harsh,
that even the spider lily blooming

on the windowsill seems no more
than another promise, soon to be broken.

It is like a lover who speaks
the passionate language of fidelity, but

when you look for him, there he is
in the arms of winter.

ZEPHYR

The three slender poplar trees
outside my window, almost joined
at the root, reminded me
of the three Graces in Botticelli's
"Allegory of Spring," even their fragile leaves
looking somehow like Renaissance hair.
So today when a stiff wind snapped
one of them in half, I wondered
if the other two would feel bereft,
as I did, debris of leaf and twig
burying their delicate feet.

Ridiculous of course. And anyway
it's the design I'll miss,
the way the three of them together
balanced the composition.
How could I know that Botticelli's Cupid
pointing his mischievous arrows
wasn't as dangerous as Zephyr—
fat cheeks blown out in windy fury?
That wind has reached across the canvas
in squalls and hurricanes, all the way
here to these Maryland hills.

Deer Fence

Inside the new deer fence
wildflowers, absent for years,
cover our hill again with half-forgotten
flecks of white, like so many
ghosts of themselves
on the dark floor of the forest.
I pick a bunch: tooth wort,
and Dutchman's-breeches,
so luminous with mystery
we must tame them with the names
of household things.
But where are the deer now?
What other woman's flowers
fill their mouths with
the soft colors of spring?

Snowdrops

Frozen fast
to their stems,
the snowdrops

are small bells
without clappers, songs
without words.

The namesakes
of blizzard
and flake,

they hang
their white
heads,

presiding
over the slow
death of winter.

SHADBLOW

Because the shad
are swimming
in our waters now,

breaching the skin
of the river with their
tarnished silvery fins,

heading upstream
straight for our tables
where already

knives and forks gleam
in anticipation, these trees
in the woods break

into flower—small, white
flags surrendering
to the season.

SAD

Is it seasonal affective disorder
I suffer from? This special lamp
I bought doesn't help at all,
but I do light up whenever
the sun itself appears. You say
the blossoms are most themselves
on a cloudy day, as if contrast
is what flowers are about.
But I feel as swollen with useless tears
as the clouds must be with rain,
projecting their shadows
over fields that are simply waiting
to blaze back to green.

The world is always going to pieces,
and we're all growing rapidly
towards our deaths, even the children.
But just one hit of sun,
one almost lethal shot
of pure, yellow light
(like the hand of some saint
I don't even believe in
touching my face)
and I'll forget the whole broken world,
forget the impermanence of beauty.
I'll simply catch on fire from
a single spoke of sun.

Cyclone

With a broom as tall as he is,
a boy is swatting the dogwood petals
from the tree his mother planted,
is sweeping them from every branch until
they swarm like small butterflies
around his head, littering the grass
like tissue party favors.
Is it anger at his mother, at the tree,
that moves him, or is it an ecstasy
of power, his mad ability
to make this bounty of pink blossoms shower
over his hair and his flailing arms?
Now his mother comes to the door
and her astonishment is partly rage,
partly inadvertent pleasure at the storm
of color falling like pastel snow
from her tree. She stares at her son
with perfect incomprehension
of all that lies ahead of them.

Rose

What are they hiding,
these fleshy layers, smooth
as the skins

of an onion,
and in their own way
equally pungent?

Here in a simple vase
in a simple room
evening enters,

and all other color fades
until only the rose
glows—red

as the tip of a cigarette:
a fist of petals
each as separate

as any other
mortal keeper
of secrets.

LEAVING THE ISLAND

We roll up rugs and strip the beds by rote,
summer expires as it has done before.
The ferry is no simple pleasure boat

nor are we simply cargo, though we'll float
alongside heavy trucks—their stink and roar.
We roll up rugs and strip the beds by rote.

This bit of land whose lines the glaciers wrote
becomes the muse of memory once more;
the ferry is no simple pleasure boat.

I'll trade my swimsuit for a woolen coat;
the torch of autumn has but small allure.
We roll up rugs and strip the beds by rote.

The absences these empty shells denote
suggest the losses winter has in store.
The ferry is no simple pleasure boat.

The songs of summer dwindle to one note:
the fog horn's blast (which drowns this closing door).
We rolled up rugs and stripped the beds by rote.
The ferry is no simple pleasure boat.

V

THE GREAT DOG OF NIGHT

John Wilde, oil on panel

The great dog of night
growls at the windows,
barks at the door.

Soon I must straddle
its sleek back and fly
over the fields

and rooftops
of sleep, above us
a vague moon

loose in the sky,
far ahead of us
morning.

Fever Dream

Lying on a deck chair,
under the weight
of the consuming sun,
I watch the shoreline of health

as it recedes in the distance.
I am nearly used up—
a lit match burning down
to my own fingertips;

an old book, once brimming
with language, whose splayed pages
shrivel to ash. What is left
is the smell of salt

and the momentum of the tide
which like a restless animal
carries me on its back, away
from this simmering heat

towards the sheer edge
of the inhabitable world.

Thought Upon Waking

What if this ordinary morning
I am waking to (sun tangled
in curtains . . . a confusion
of birds at the window . . .
the scented grace of coffee)
is merely a memory
of some other morning years ago?
What if I turn my head

and you are not beside me,
haven't been for years,
and there is only the whiteout
of your vacant pillow?
This is either fact or prophecy—
my one life no more than a spool
of memories unwinding
into the unpersuaded air.

ENCORE
FOR RF

Before you go,
I would like to reprise for you
the blue cloud in the song's first stanza

and my own tears halfway down the page
which mark the score in half notes
or footprints in the disappearing distance.

I can still hear applause—that winter thunder,
but let's forget the audience
some of whom are heading for the doors.

Let the violins be silent, their bows
like so many lopped branches
on the tree outside your frosted window.

Let all the fingers sleep
on the polished keys of all the pianos.
Let only percussions be left—

a cymbal like the bronze sun setting;
a drum beating time
to the fading pulse in your neck.

Rivermist
for Roland Flint

When the kennel where my ridgeback died
some thirty years ago, wrote
to ask for my business again,
offering us one free night's board
for every three nights paid, I looked
at that name on the envelope: Rivermist,
imagining they were writing to say
that Mowgli was somehow alive,
the swordlike blade of fur still bristling
on his back; that he had waited
all these years for me to pick him up.
And though I've had four dogs since,
a small one at my feet right now, each
running too swiftly through his life and mine,
I could have wept, thinking of rivers and mists—
how in their wavering shadows
they had prefigured and concealed
the losses to come: mother and uncles, friends,
and Roland now, so newly dead, who
on the flyleaf of an early book once wrote,
in his careful, redemptive hand: with love
for Linda and Ira, and for Mowgli.

Death Is Intended

"On Feb. 6, 67 year old Guy Waterman, naturalist, outdoorsman, devoted husband . . . decided to climb a New Hampshire mountain, lie down on the cold stones and die overnight of exposure. 'Death is intended,' he wrote." —*The New York Times Book Review*

". . . the melancholy beauty of giving it all up." —Robert Hass

Isn't that what Eskimos did when they were old,
dragged themselves through a wilderness
of ice and up some mountain?
Then they could fall asleep forever,
their dark eyes speckled with falling snow—
not suicide exactly, but the opening
of a door so death could enter.
"Quit while you're ahead," my father told me
as I was feeding quarters into slot machines.
And that's what Waterman did, he quit
before infirmity could catch him, or other afflictions
whose breath he could already smell.
But I wanted more: a waterfall of coins
spilt on my lap, the raw, electric charge
of money. I came away with nothing;
but I still want more, if only more chapters
in the family book I'm part of: I want
to read all the unfolding stories, each child
a mystery only time can solve.
Was it bravery or cowardice what Waterman did,
or are those simply two sides of a coin,
like the coin some casual God might flip,
deciding who would live or die that day?
I'd rather flip the coin myself, but not at 67.
And not quite yet at 70, as spring
streams in over our suburban hills, enflaming
even the white New Hampshire mountains.

Remembering Frost
at Kennedy's Inauguration

Even the flags seemed frozen
to their poles, and the men
stamping their well-shod feet
resembled an army of overcoats.

But we were young and fueled
by hope, our ardor burned away
the cold. We were the president's,
and briefly the president would be ours.

The old poet stumbled
over his own indelible words,
his breath a wreath around his face:
a kind of prophecy.

September 11, 2001

I have been listening to disaster
on the radio all day long
and sometimes on television.

Outside the trees are unbelievably
green, autumn has hardly begun
its devastations.

I think of the albums of war
with their backdrops of charred trees,
their broken landscapes,

while here the various beauties
of the world
display themselves,

the September sky retains
a mocking,
pristine blue.

And the Pandora's box on my table
spills the colors of carnage
all over the room.

Apple Season in a Time of War

The children are terrible
in their innocence,
and the frightened parents
can neither scold nor protect them

as the leaves continue to fall
like tiny portents
from the ancestral trees.
Weather is all

that remains unchanged,
with its accidental
almost merciful cruelties,
its winds, its falling temperatures.

But I can hear the children
whose laughter rings
like small but dangerous
hammers on an anvil.

I can hear the buzz of radio voices,
persistent as insects
on all the frequencies
of madness.

What We Are Capable Of

On Reading of Prisoner Abuse at Abu Ghraib

What we are capable of
is always astonishing,
though never quite a surprise.

"Astronomers find more evidence
of dark matter," the newspaper says
on the next page—a fact or metaphor?

I think of those villagers in France
who risked their only lives
to save a handful of Jews, and I try

to find from that fading chink of light
an incandescent path
through all these darknesses.

Landscape Near Dachau

Adolf Holzel, circa 1900

This is the innocence of blue—
pale blue sky, a blue river,
and of white—
snow unsullied yet
by human history.
See the farmhouses:
their humble roofs,
their chimneys.
The only shadows
are the shadows
of trees, wavering
on the pastel water.

AT THE UDVAR-HAZY AIRPLANE MUSEUM, CHANTILLY, VIRGINIA

Here in this cavernous space
old airmen in leather jackets
as creased
as their faces, wander
from plane to plane

the way Odysseus might have,
back in Ithaca, moving
from ship to wrecked ship,
eyeing a statue of Circe,
naked behind glass;

or Icarus revisiting his wings—
reading the text above them and thinking:
so that's what the problem was,
the melting point of wax.

Here the Focke-Wulf, the Kawasaki Toryu,
the Enola Gay stand wing to wing
like killer bees, their stingers removed,
and harmless now
as the model planes of children.

Here real children line up
to experience weightlessness,
not the kind their grandfathers
are feeling—
the heaviness of time

momentarily suspended—
but the kind the astronauts know,
a feeling as curious as the romance
of war that lingers here
in the photographs of heroes:

Rickenbacker, his white
silk scarf blowing
behind him like a windsock,
wearing his leather helmet
as though it were a crown.

Isn't the moon dark too,
most of the time?

And doesn't the white page
seem unfinished

without the dark stain
of alphabets?

When God demanded light,
he didn't banish darkness.

Instead he invented
ebony and crows

and that small mole
on your left cheekbone.

Or did you mean to ask
"Why are you sad so often?"

Ask the moon.
Ask what it has witnessed.

A Rainy Country

"Je suis comme le roi d'un pays pluvieux"—Baudelaire

The headlines and feature stories alike
leak blood all over the breakfast table,
the wounding of the world mingling
with smells of bacon and bread.

Small pains are merely anterooms for larger,
and every shadow has a brother, just waiting.
Even grace is sullied by ancient angers.
I must remember it has always been like this:

those Trojan women, learning their fates;
the simple sharpness of the guillotine.
A filigree of cruelty adorns every culture.
I've thumbed through the pages of my life,

longing for childhood whose failures
were merely personal, for all
the stations of love I passed through.
Shadows and the shadow of shadows.

I am like the queen of a rainy country,
powerless and grown old. Another morning
with its quaint obligations: newspaper,
bacon grease, rattle of dishes and bones.